I WANT TO BE... Book Series
Creator/Producer: Stephanie Maze, Maze Productions, Inc.
Writer and Educational Consultant: Catherine O'Neill Grace
Designer: Alexandra Littlehales

Photographers for I WANT TO BE A FIREFIGHTER
Annie Griffiths Belt; Nicole Bengevino;
Lara Jo Regan; Richard Nowitz;
Stephen Ringman; Michael Gallacher

Other books available in this series:
I WANT TO BE AN ASTRONAUT
I WANT TO BE A CHEF
I WANT TO BE A DANCER
I WANT TO BE AN ENGINEER
I WANT TO BE A VETERINARIAN

Requests for permission to make copies
of any part of the work should be mailed to:
Permissions Department, Harcourt Brace & Company,
6277 Sea Harbor Drive, Orlando, Florida 32887-6777.

Photography credits appear on page 48.

Library of Congress Cataloging-in-Publication Data
Maze, Stephanie.
I want to be a firefighter/created by Stephanie Maze/written by Catherine O'Neill Grace.
p. cm.—(I want to be—book series)
"A Maze Productions book."
Summary: Describes the different jobs done by people working
in the fire-fighting profession and some people who have
made important contributions in this field.
ISBN 0-15-201865-4 ISBN 0-15-201937-5 pb
1. Fire extinction—Vocational guidance—Juvenile literature.
2. Fire prevention—Vocational guidance—Juvenile literature.
3. Fire fighters—Juvenile literature. [1. Fire extinction—Vocational guidance. 2. Fire prevention—Vocational guidance. 3. Fire fighters. 4. Occupations]
I. Grace, Catherine O'Neill, 1950– .
II. Title. III. Series.
TH9119.M39 1999
363.37'023—dc21 98-8270

First edition
A C E F D B
A C E F D B (pb)

Film processing by A & I Color, Los Angeles
Pre-press through PrintNet
Printed and bound by Tien Wah Press, Singapore

I Want to Be...

A FIREFIGHTER

A Maze Productions Book

HARCOURT BRACE & COMPANY

SAN DIEGO   NEW YORK   LONDON

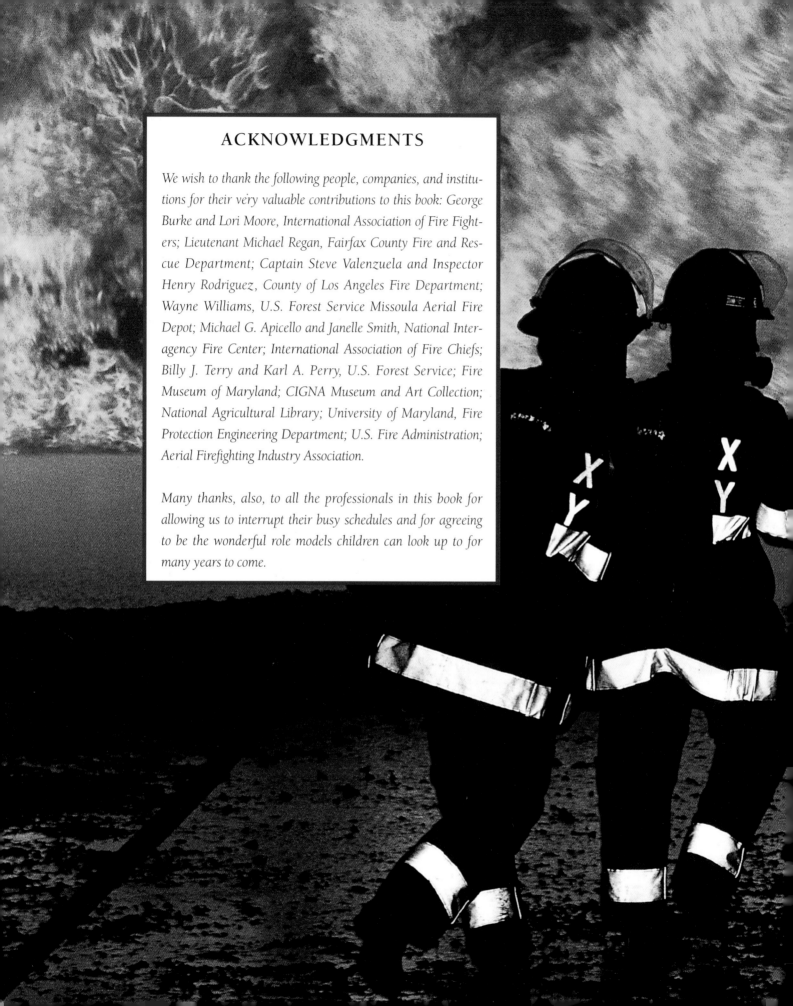

ACKNOWLEDGMENTS

We wish to thank the following people, companies, and institutions for their very valuable contributions to this book: George Burke and Lori Moore, International Association of Fire Fighters; Lieutenant Michael Regan, Fairfax County Fire and Rescue Department; Captain Steve Valenzuela and Inspector Henry Rodriguez, County of Los Angeles Fire Department; Wayne Williams, U.S. Forest Service Missoula Aerial Fire Depot; Michael G. Apicello and Janelle Smith, National Interagency Fire Center; International Association of Fire Chiefs; Billy J. Terry and Karl A. Perry, U.S. Forest Service; Fire Museum of Maryland; CIGNA Museum and Art Collection; National Agricultural Library; University of Maryland, Fire Protection Engineering Department; U.S. Fire Administration; Aerial Firefighting Industry Association.

Many thanks, also, to all the professionals in this book for allowing us to interrupt their busy schedules and for agreeing to be the wonderful role models children can look up to for many years to come.

To all children who dream the impossible dreams

Where to Start

Do you stay calm in emergencies? Do you enjoy activities that require strength and stamina? Can you make split-second decisions? Do you like to help people? If so, you may have what it takes to be a firefighter, one of the most demanding, dangerous—and important—jobs in the world. Firefighters save lives and property, often while putting their own lives at risk.

When a fire starts, most people try to get away from the smoke and flames—but a firefighter must step right in. At right, firefighter Bret Underhill works in the midst of a wind-driven blaze that started in a large garbage dump at the Salt River Indian Reservation in Arizona. Fire-resistant gear protects him from the flames. He will use his shovel to mound dirt on the flames to smother them. Other firefighters will assist him, since teamwork is very important when extinguishing blazes.

Firefighters work in cities and in rural areas, in suburbs and in parklands—wherever there may be a danger of fire. Some are volunteers; others are paid professionals. Besides battling blazes, they rescue victims from life-threatening situations, provide help in medical emergencies, and educate people about fire prevention and safety. Every day, while we go about our lives, firefighters are on alert, ready to jump into action to protect us and the places we love.

Emergency medical technicians

Deputy fire chief

RALSTON ENG
CO1

From phones to fires. *Fire fighting (large photo above) involves leaders like Deputy Fire Chief Robert Lee of the Los Angeles County Fire Department (left), emergency medical technicians (above left), and calm dispatchers like Angela Mitchell (above right). During "down time," a firefighter (right) cleans a fire truck in Mendham Township, New Jersey.*

Dispatcher

Firefighter

Urban Firefighters

Fighting fires in urban areas—where large numbers of people live together, often in older buildings—is a real challenge. It requires the teamwork of many people—from the fire chief, who is in charge of hiring, training, and deploying firefighters, to the dispatchers, who answer emergency calls and use computer technology to locate and send help fast! The firefighters in the large photo at left work together to battle a blaze in Mendham, New Jersey.

Some urban fire departments are very large. For example, in Los Angeles County, California, nearly 3,500 firefighters provide fire and emergency services to the 3½ million citizens who live within the sprawling city's boundaries. The department's 147 fire stations receive some 400,000 emergency calls each year. About one-third are for fires—including brush fires in the dry hills surrounding the city. The rest are for incidents that require assistance from emergency medical technicians (EMTs). These calls might be for traffic accidents or medical emergencies such as heart attacks.

Urban firefighters have to be ready for anything. They put out fires in high-rise apartment buildings, factories, and houses; they rescue people from crushed vehicles after traffic accidents; they inspect buildings to help prevent fires from ever getting started; they educate school-children. They help to keep whole cities safe.

9

Seattle Fire Station No. 10

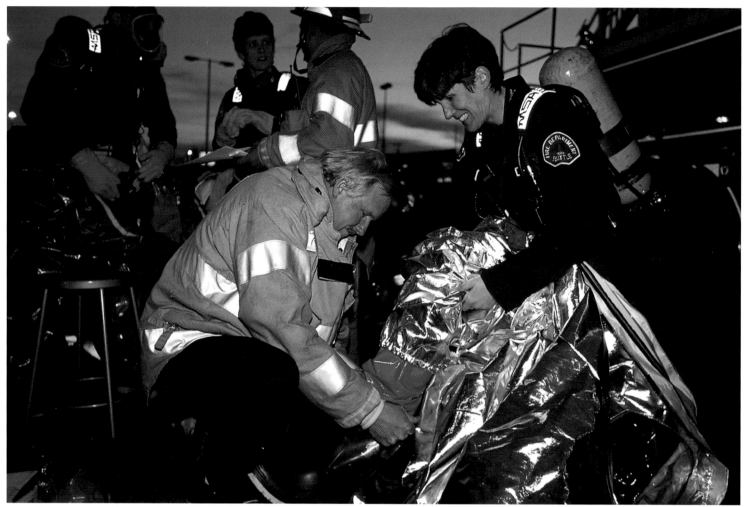

Working at Seattle's Fire Station No. 10 is an around-the-clock job. The firefighters work 24-hour shifts, eating and living at the fire station while they're on duty. They must be ready to go at any time of day or night.

Fire Station No. 10 is one of 34 stations that serve the 525,000 residents who live within the city limits of Seattle, Washington. This station is located downtown and houses Seattle's special hazardous-materials, or "haz-mat," van. When toxic chemicals spill, the van is called into action. Above, at the scene of a spill, Inger Bakken gets help from Bill Mitchell in putting on a haz-mat suit. The suit is designed to protect firefighters from burns that corrosive chemicals can cause. The tank on her back contains oxygen to breathe in case the chemicals give off toxic fumes. Firefighters must always be prepared for the worst. Luckily, this was a relatively minor detergent spill.

Meanwhile, things are quieter at the

firehouse—at least for a time. When they're not responding to emergencies, firefighters maintain their equipment at the fire station—and wait. At bottom left, facing page, Chuck Seeman prepares dinner, meat loaf, for the firefighters on duty. He's on duty, too. In fact, he had to interrupt his meal preparations to answer a call.

Fire Station No. 10 has an excellent response rate. The average time from when an emergency call comes into the station from the dispatcher until firefighters reach the scene of the emergency is 3.7 minutes. Some calls are false alarms, and many emergencies turn out to be medical calls. (Like most firefighters, Seattle firefighters must be certified as emergency medical technicians). Below left, Firehouse No. 10 firefighters join paramedics helping a man who is having convulsions. The firefighters are wearing blue shirts; the paramedics wear white ones.

Fire fighting is exhausting work, so after any type of call, Roger Bianchi is relieved to remove his heavy equipment and sit down for the return ride to the firehouse (below right). Back at Fire Station No. 10, a hot meat-loaf dinner is waiting.

Be prepared. *A snowstorm means that the crew at Seattle Fire Station No. 10 must make more preparations than usual to be ready to go when a call comes in. Todd Wernet first shovels the station's driveway and then puts chains on the ladder truck's huge tires (photos above), so the truck won't skid as it speeds off to an emergency*

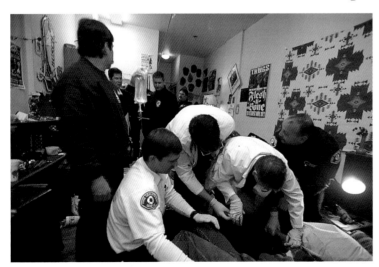

Wildland Fire Fighting

Wildland fires happen every year in forests and parkland throughout the world. Wildfires usually begin naturally when lightning strikes, but they may be set by careless campers or even arsonists. When wildfires burn out of control they can cause terrible damage. But fire can serve an ecological purpose. Flames get rid of underbrush and fallen leaves, giving trees the space they need to grow. Small fires can keep ecosystems healthy and prevent larger, more serious forest fires by minimizing a fire's natural fuel.

In the United States, the National Interagency Fire Center (NIFC), in Boise, Idaho, maintains a research and support facility for wildland fire fighting. NIFC experts specialize in fields such as fire behavior, fire technology, aviation, and meteorology. Specialists at the center monitor wildland fires and decide how to manage them. They often consult maps and check temperatures to predict how a wildland fire will move (facing page, small photos, bottom).

Firefighters use special methods to battle wildland blazes. Hand crews try to slow wildfires by creating "firelines"—clean trenches around the edge of a fire—and by clearing brush by hand or with small, controlled blazes (facing page, small photos, top left and center). Members of "hotshot" crews work right inside fires. In the large photo at left, Turner Brooks of the Fort Apache Hotshots sets a controlled fire to burn brush in Idaho. After a fire, engine crews "mop up" smoldering spots (facing page, top right).

Help from above. *Aircraft play a vital role in wildland fire fighting. A helicopter drops water on a fire from a tank suspended from its belly (above left). A large air tanker releases chemical retardant to slow the spread of a fire (above center). Wildland firefighters rappel on ropes dangling from a helicopter into a remote area to fight fires started by lightning (above right).*

Smokejumper Training

The firefighters on these pages may look like they are flying into a war—and in a way they are. They are smokejumpers, and they wage war against fire in remote forests.

This specialized method of fire fighting began officially in 1940 when a raging blaze spread through the Nez Perce National Forest in Idaho. There were no roads into the forest and hiking in would have taken too long, so firefighters had to find another way to reach the flames. The U.S. Forest Service had already been sending fire-fighters into forests on practice jumps. In Idaho the method was tested in action—and the

smokejumping service was born. Some of the first smokejumpers were airplane stuntmen and World War I veteran aviators. Those pioneers rescued large areas of precious forest. Ever since, smokejumping has been an important weapon for fighting wildland fires.

Today smokejumpers are professionals who train rigorously to stay in top condition while they hone their parachuting and fire-fighting skills. The smokejumpers above—trainees from a base in Missoula, Montana—hold their para-chutes as they head off for a practice jump. At near right, one trainee leaps from a plane, as he learns to land on smaller and smaller target sites. Precision becomes a matter of life or death when you're leaping into a forest fire.

Smokejumping is physically grueling. A firefighter carries lots of equipment, including a hard hat with a head lamp, a main and a reserve parachute, and several Pulaski axes. Extra equipment, tools, and water are dropped in cargo boxes at the fire scene. After the battle is over, smokejumpers often have to hike long distances to get back to camp.

Today there are some four hundred smokejumpers. The next time you and your family enjoy a national park, remember the daring work they do to keep the land green, beautiful, and safe.

Ready, set, jump! Trainees learn parachuting skills One drill strengthens the upper body and teaches trainees to steer their 'chutes (top). Smokejumpers also learn to land in water (above), a move they later master from the air. Because they jump into forests, it's important for smokejumpers to learn how to get untangled from a tree (near left).

Education

Would you know what to do if your clothes caught on fire? What if an earthquake hit while you were at school? Students who participate in the school programs shown on these pages know how to protect themselves. They have learned important survival skills from fire-fighters—and that knowledge could someday save their lives.

Many fire-fighting and safety organizations run programs for kids. At Madison Elementary School in Pomona, California, students learn how to cover their heads and necks and how to find the safest places for shelter during an earth-quake (top right). A third grader (large photo, facing page) demonstrates the "stop, drop, and roll" technique for her classmates.

Each year more than fifteen thousand Ameri-cans are seriously burned when their clothes catch fire. Sometimes these burns are made worse because victims panic and run. Fire needs oxygen to burn, and the breeze a person gener-ates by running feeds the fire. If your clothes ever catch fire, do not run. First *stop*. Then *drop* to the floor. Protect your face with your hands, and *roll* over and over to smother the fire. Don't stop rolling until the flames have been extin-guished.

Project Rescue pairs professional firefighters with middle schoolers interested in a fire-fighting career. In Los Angeles, a firefighter who works for Project Rescue shows his helmet to his student partner (center right).

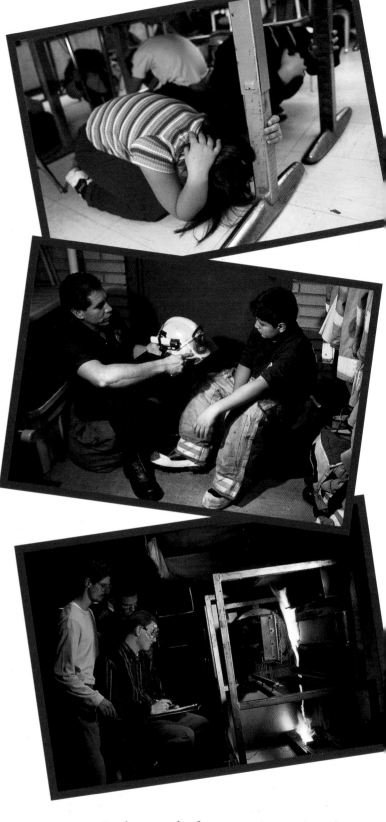

Fire power. *Students in the fire protection engineering program at the University of Maryland in College Park study how flames behave (above). Eventually this knowl-edge may help them to make more effective tools to detect and fight fire. The university is one of the few in the world that offers undergraduate degrees in fire-protection science.*

Hands on. *At Waterloo Elementary School in Columbia, Maryland, a fire department representative uses the Kids' Safety House, a mobile home fitted with a smoke machine, to teach the right way to escape smoke by staying low (above left) and about danger spots such as fireplaces (above right). Students in the Montgomery County, Maryland, high school fire science program—which teaches emergency medical techniques and fire fighting—practice bandaging (above center).*

Other Programs

Part of a firefighter's mission is to educate the community, which can mean teaching accident prevention. High school students look on as firefighters demonstrate emergency medical care during a simulated "prom night" accident in Fairfax County, Virginia (facing page, top). The firefighters use a special brace to immobilize the head and spine of the accident "victim'" just as they would if she had been hurt in a real crash. This accident-prevention program is designed to discourage the students from drinking and driving by graphically illustrating the possible consequences of mixing the two.

Firefighters in departments throughout the United States consider community service an essential part of their job. In Los Angeles County firefighters are required to do community service—so being able to communicate effectively is an important job qualification.

The public-service programs that firefighters put on often involve teaching young people skills that firefighters use on the job. For example, at top left, a Los Angeles teenager learns cardiopulmonary resuscitation (CPR) during summer lifeguard training. (The "victim" is a dummy.) The Los Angeles County Fire Department Lifeguard Operations Unit teaches beach and ocean safety skills, first aid, lifesaving, and CPR to kids ages nine to seventeen. At the end of the six-week course, participants are certified as junior lifeguards.

Wheel of safety. *At the county fair in Fairfax, Virginia, kids watch as a firefighter twirls a wheel that provides information about smoke detectors and other methods of fire prevention (above). Firefighters work at this fair not just because it's fun. Teaching families about fire safety—especially how to install and correctly use smoke detectors—saves lives. A working smoke detector doubles a person's chance of surviving a blaze.*

Practice drills. *Explorer Scouts, boys ages sixteen to twenty-one, learn about emergency medical procedures from a Los Angeles County Fire Department paramedic (right). Using a real emergency medical kit, the Scouts practice the steps EMTs take to stabilize the condition of an accident "victim," another Scout who's pretending to need emergency treatment.*

Basic Training

The emergency scenes on these pages are all in a day's work for firefighting trainees at the Fire and Rescue Academy in Fairfax, Virginia. The students pictured here participate in "incident simulations" designed to develop skills they will need on the job. The training is crucial. In emergency situations, the quick action of these men and women can mean the difference between life and death.

Before they began training, these candidates had to meet the Fairfax County requirements for becoming a firefighter: They are all at least nineteen years old, have a high school diploma or its equivalent, and have been drug free for the past year. After passing the written test, completing a 1½-mile run in thirteen minutes or less, and undergoing medical and psychological evaluations, they began training to become firefighters.

It's hot, hard work. Above, a firefighter-in-training learns to direct a jet of water at a

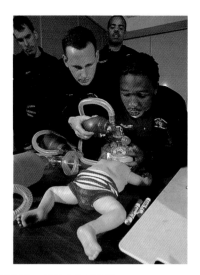

Breath of life. *Firefighters learn medical procedures so they can respond to all emergencies. Fire trucks carry medical equipment, such as the respirator these trainees try out on a dummy of a baby (right). This device helps a person who has inhaled smoke or has stopped breathing for some other reason.*

burning building with the help of classmates. A fire hose shoots out water with incredible force; it takes skill (and sometimes assistance!) to direct the water where it will do the most good.

To be a firefighter you have to be strong. Firefighters often have to lift heavy equipment in addition to the eighty pounds of gear they typically carry (small photo, facing page). Handling ladders safely is an important skill, since firefighters frequently climb onto roofs or through windows to reach the source of the flames.

Sometimes firefighters may be called on to rescue victims from swiftly moving water or from the upper stories of burning buildings. Trainees in Fairfax are taught water-rescue techniques (above) and learn to rappel down a wall using ropes (right center). They also practice quickly putting on special equipment such as a mask and air tank (right).

Firefighter candidates must be courageous, strong, and agile. They must also possess incredible endurance, good judgment, and compassion for others. Now can you see why?

Specialties

Disasters can happen anywhere. Some fire-fighters undertake extra training so they will be able to cope with the special demands of certain emergencies.

Because Los Angeles is in an earthquake zone, some of its firefighters learn to perform unusual rescues. Firefighters practice a "high-angle" rescue drill using ropes and other climbing gear (right center). If an earthquake hits the city, its firefighters will be ready to help people as needed in all kinds of places. In the large photo at right, a Los Angeles County firefighter descends into a narrow well as he practices a "confined-space" rescue. The city's fire department also trains specialists in scuba diving (far right, top), which is used in underwater search-and-rescue missions.

Weather disasters such as tornadoes may require firefighters to find people in collapsed buildings. Firefighters practice search-and-rescue techniques with the help of a dog trained to locate victims in debris in Fairfax County, Virginia (top right). Fairfax County fire department also trains some firefighters in hazardous-materials containment. At far right center, fire-fighters in haz-mat suits climb aboard a railway car venting toxic smoke. The equipment and materials used to put out fires caused by toxic materials depend on the chemicals involved; the firefighters' special training prepares them to make the right decisions.

Danger, aviation fuel! *These pictures show what happens when aircraft fuel ignites. At bottom left, marine firefighters battle a blaze that erupted when a tanker carrying millions of gallons of aviation fuel collided with another vessel in Tampa, Florida. Air Force firefighters in haz-mat suits spray chemical foam on jet-fuel flames that water can't put out (right).*

Fire-Fighting Vocabulary

Fire fighting is a profession that has always involved specialized equipment and methods. Some tools, such as buckets and axes, have remained important through the ages. Other gear has come into use more recently as technology has improved. Here are some modern tools and techniques considered essential by today's firefighters.

SELF-CONTAINED BREATHING APPARATUS

Firefighters often encounter smoke or fumes that may endanger their health—and even their lives. When that happens, they need clean air to breathe immediately. That's why all firefighters carry SCBAs, which deliver oxygen through a face mask. A well-trained firefighter can put on this gear—a mask, several hoses, and an air tank in a backpack—in less than three minutes. SCBAs save firefighters from smoke inhalation every day.

DISPATCHING TERMINAL

Most fire departments operate centers to monitor emergencies. Calls to fire, rescue, or 911 are routed to the closest dispatcher by a computer. Trained dispatchers answer the call and use the dispatching terminal to send the appropriate personnel and equipment to the scene. With systems like this, citizens waste no time finding the right help and firefighters can respond more quickly than ever to emergencies.

MONITOR

When battling blazes in tall buildings, a monitor—a fixed-in-place fire hose and nozzle capable of spraying water under very high pressure—comes in handy. Also called a deck gun when positioned on top of a fire truck, it can be used to direct a steady stream of water at flames in high, hard-to-reach places. A firefighter regulates the flow of water by adjusting the deck gun's nozzle.

INFLATABLE ZUMRO TENT

This decontamination shelter can be used when firefighters are exposed to hazardous materials in the field. It consists of an inflatable frame with an inner canopy, floor, and built-in shower. The tent can be up and ready to use in just two minutes. Then firefighters whose protective "haz-mat" suits have been contaminated by toxic materials may step inside to get cleaned off without spreading the hazardous materials.

VENTILATION

Smoke rises to the top of a burning building. Firefighters often use saws and axes to break a hole through the roof. This venting process releases smoke and flames trapped within the building. Clearing the smoke makes it easier to fight the fire and rescue people who may be caught inside the burning structure.

PUMP PANEL

By looking at these gauges, the firefighter who operates this equipment knows exactly how many thousands of gallons of water are being pumped through the hoses and at what pressure. Many pump panels have controls that allow an operator to rotate the valve on a fire hose to change the angle and pressure of the water flow so it can be directed at different parts of a blaze.

FOAM

Firefighters use chemical foam to extinguish flames caused by explosive substances like gasoline, or aviation fuel. A blanket of foam can put out these fires and prevent explosions. Firefighters undergo special training to learn to apply a thick, even coat of foam to smother flames and to keep charred material from smoldering.

FUSEE

This firefighter uses a fusee—a fire-lighter on a pole—to start a "prescribed burn." Regular small fires, set on purpose, help control the buildup of debris and speed up the recycling of dead plant material into soil nutrients. Prescribed burns are also used to create areas to stop wildfires by removing the fuel they need to burn.

DRIP TORCH

Experts who manage "prescribed burns"—fires that are purposely set to clear underbrush or to keep wildfires from advancing—make use of this tool. The hand-held can holds a mixture of gasoline and diesel fuel. A firefighter dribbles modest amounts of the flammable liquid on small areas of brush to create a line of flame that can be easily controlled.

RETARDANT

This reddish-orange material can help slow the spread of forest fires. Specially trained pilots drop huge loads of the substance—a mixture of chemicals, thickening gum, and colored water, about twice as thick as molasses—from airplanes. The color helps pilots determine whether they have hit the target and makes the material visible to firefighters on the ground.

History of Fire Fighting

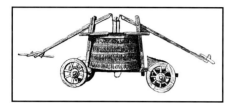

For as long as people have gathered in communities to live, they have used fire for cooking food and heating homes. And since ancient times, people have found ways to fight fires that got out of control. Fire brigades go back almost six thousand years in China alone!

At first fire-fighting technology was simple, but it developed quickly. Ancient Romans stored water in wooden tubs to put out fires. The heavy tubs had to be carried to the fire, where simple pumps propelled water through a tube turned toward the flames.

Medieval Europeans relied on wooden or leather buckets to carry water to extinguish fires (usually to little avail). In medieval European cities, people were terrified of fire, partly because they lived so close together, often in houses constructed of highly flammable materials such as wood and thatch. Many hundred years later, fire tubs like the ones used by the Romans reappeared in Europe with a significant improvement—they had wheels (above left).

In the American colonies, each household kept leather buckets on hand to use to fight flames. When the colonists heard someone cry "Fire!" they threw their empty buckets into the street. Volunteers raced by, gathering the buckets along the way to the scene of the fire. There they

Early efforts. *At right, Saint Florian, the patron saint of fire prevention, douses flames using a method popular in the sixteenth century. In the seventeenth-century engraving below, women rush to fill a barrel with water as men use a hand-operated piston to extinguish the fire.*

Ready to fight. *Rival nineteenth-century volunteer companies raced to be the first to reach a fire (above). A nineteenth-century fireman pulls a hose reel out of a firehouse (right). An illustration, titled "The Ruins" (below) shows the aftermath of a city blaze in 1854.*

formed "bucket brigades"—a line of people (sometimes even kids!) that stretched from a water source, such as a pond or a cistern, to the fire. They passed filled buckets from hand to hand, and those standing closest to the flames threw the water on the fire.

Later, in the 1700s, colonists began to use wheeled tubs like those in Europe. On the facing page, third photo from top, children and other citizens participate in a "bucket brigade" to fight a blaze in a wooden house.

Colonists also assembled firefighters to protect their property in the New World. Benjamin Franklin (facing page, bottom left) was the first American volunteer fire chief. He founded the Union Fire Company in Pennsylvania in 1742. Other volunteer fire companies followed.

In the nineteenth century, firefighters began organizing themselves into rival clubs and associations and participating in civic events like parades. The small picture at bottom right on the facing page shows early-nineteenth-century firefighters before a parade outside one of the first fire stations in the United States, the Hibernia Engine Company No. 1, in Philadelphia.

Many fire-fighting groups were supported by insurance payments that residents made to the companies. Houses bore shields from specific companies, which would extinguish fires only at homes that carried their insurance. Competition was fierce!

American firefighters relied on hand-pumped fire engines such as the one in the illustration at near left well into the nineteenth century.

Some nineteenth-century fire engines were so large they needed two dozen men to move them (top left). Horses were also used to rush equipment to fires (top center).

In the mid-1800s a revolutionary invention—the steam engine—changed fire fighting. These machines harnessed the energy of steam to power water pumps (top right). The pumps could spray from three hundred to twelve hundred gallons of water per minute, depending on their size. The steam-driven fire engine soon became the most important piece of fire equipment and remained vital into the twentieth century. The last steam fire engine was manufactured in 1914, but steam-powered fire equipment continued to be used to fight fire—like the 1918 blaze in Washington, D.C., (bottom, near right).

Another invention, the gasoline-powered internal combustion engine, changed fire fighting again in the 1920s. Before long, horse-drawn steam engines were replaced by motorized fire trucks that carried a pump, a chemical tank for putting out small fires, and a long fire hose. At the scene of a fire, firefighters attached the hose to a fire hydrant linked to water mains far underground. For the first time firefighters had an unlimited supply of water.

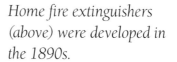

Home fire extinguishers (above) were developed in the 1890s.

Equipment advances. *The alarm box (below) was invented in the 1850s. A working alarm might have prevented the Great Fire of Chicago (above), which burned 17,000 buildings in 1871.*

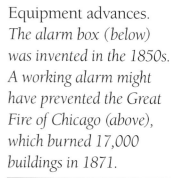

Diversity. *From Colonial times, African Americans as well as women fought fires. In 1919 the firefighters of Engine Company No. 4 in Maryland were black (above)—except their captain. Long Beach, New York, had an all-female volunteer fire department in the 1920s.*

By the early twentieth century, firefighters had become trained professionals. Their leaders formed the International Association of Firefighters (IAFF), one of the earliest labor unions (organizations of workers) in the United States. The IAFF's founder and first president, Thomas Spellacy (facing page, bottom right), began the fight to ensure fair working conditions for firefighters, including women such as Anne Crawford Allen Holst (near left) who became the first female fire chief in Cedar Hill, Rhode Island—and in the world—in 1931.

Today fire trucks have automatic ladders, advanced communication systems, and engines that can pump as much as two thousand gallons of water per minute (bottom left). Firefighters even use helicopters (bottom right). Better firefighting methods, fire-resistant building materials, and the widespread use of smoke detectors have greatly reduced fire-related injuries and deaths, but firefighters still risk their lives each day in the line of duty.

In the past, firefighters spent most of their time battling blazes. They now devote much of their time to education, building inspections, and other preventive measures to protect us from fire.

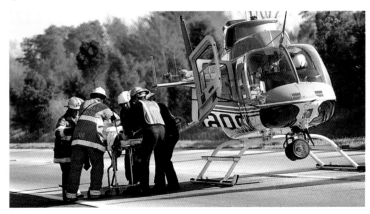

History of Wildland Fire Fighting

When forests covered much of North America, fires sparked by lightning eventually burned out on their own, often causing widespread damage. By the late 1800s, the United States had claimed the land west of the Mississippi River and relied on products from its forests and grasslands. The government set aside parks for the preservation of the country's natural beauty, and protecting this vast natural resource became a priority.

In 1872 Yellowstone National Park was founded as the first national park for "the enjoyment of the people" and for the "preservation . . . of all timber, mineral deposits, natural curiosities, or wonders." Organized protection of wildlands began there under the management of the U.S. Army.

In 1897 the General Land Office, a branch of the Department of the Interior, took over the duties of fire suppression on government wildland until the U.S. Forest Service was established in 1905. The Forest Service set up a system of lookout posts, communications stations, and military-like strategies to battle wildland blazes.

After World War I, some military aircraft were adapted for fire fighting. Pilots flew over remote

Blankets to blimps. *At top left a firefighter smothers sparks in Wallowa National Forest in Oregon in 1908. Axes, shovels, and rakes like these from 1913 (top center) are still used by wildland firefighters today. In 1921, a blimp prepares for a fire patrol over Los Angeles National Park, California (top right).*

Into the woods. *Nearly half a million unemployed people worked for the Civilian Conservation Corps to protect America's wildlands during the Great Depression of the 1930s (above). They staffed fire towers (above right, second from top) and cleared trails through forests all over the country.*

Heroes. *Above left, pioneer smokejumpers pose by their plane in 1939. African American paratroopers of the 555th B-Company were smokejumpers in World War II (above center). Women have joined the smokejumping world, too (above right)—that's Deanne Schulman and her pilot, Charlotte Lawson.*

areas to spot smoke, dumped water or chemicals on flames, and began to relay information by radio. In the 1940s planes began to drop smokejumpers into forests. Smokejumpers have saved vast areas of wildland—but there have been tragedies. In 1949 thirteen smokejumpers died in a wildfire at Mann Gulch, Montana.

After World War II, a campaign to educate the public began. You've heard of Smokey the Bear and his slogan, Only you can prevent forest fires. That's the real Smokey the Bear, a forest-fire survivor (facing page, bottom right). But forest fires still happened—including the 1988 blaze in Yellowstone that burned 45 percent of the national park (left center and bottom left).

In recent years the National Interagency Fire Center has taken over the management of wildland fires, drawing on the expertise of Native American firefighters such as the Mescalero Indians and all-female Native American crews (second from bottom, left and right). Native Americans used fire to clear land in order to prevent wildfire from spreading long before settlers ventured West. Today this practice is called "controlled burning," which is done for ecological reasons as well as to control fires.

Space-age gear. A firefighter on the Chevy Chase Fire and Rescue Squad in Maryland wears an Infrared Imaging System (IRIS) helmet, which creates an image based on differences in temperatures. The helmet lets fighters see through heavy smoke fairly clearly. The thermal imaging camera uses technology perfected during the gulf war.

High Tech

The search for new technologies to improve fire fighting continues. One recent development is the fire shelter (small photo, near left). If a wildfire approaches, a firefighter can lie down and cover his body with the shelter while the blaze races over him or her. The amazing material, made of aluminum foil bonded to fiberglass, can deflect heat up to sixteen hundred degrees Fahrenheit. At top left, the Los Angeles County Fire Department employs a high-speed computerized Fire Command and Control Facility to quickly link citizens with emergency services. The system also automatically reports, monitors, and updates information about the department's response to emergencies. Fiber-optic techniques that help doctors see inside the human body have been adapted for fire fighting. At left, second from top, a firefighter uses a fiber-optic camera to see behind concrete as he searches for survivors in an accident in Fairfax County, Virginia. The firefighters at left, second from bottom, aren't on the moon—they just look that way. Wearing protective suits and sitting in an inflatable shelter, these Fairfax County hazardous-materials specialists prepare to contain a chemical spill. At bottom left, Fairfax County EMTs demonstrate the use of a defibrillator, a machine that uses an electric shock in an attempt to restore a heartbeat in a heart attack victim.

Did You Know . . .

. . . that dogs played an important role in the search-and-rescue effort after the April 1995 bombing of the Alfred Murrah Federal Building in Oklahoma City, Oklahoma? At left, firefighter Skip Fernandez of Miami, Florida, rests his head on his partner, Aspen, a golden retriever, after finishing their twelve-hour shift. Finding survivors was dangerous work for the heroes, human and animal. One hundred sixty-eight people died in the terrorist blast.

. . . that approximately 90 percent of homes in the United States have at least one smoke detector?

. . . that some two million fires are reported in the United States every year?

. . . that careless smoking is the leading cause of fatalities in residential fires?

. . . that the fire hose was developed in the early 1800s? Made of fire-resistant leather, the first hoses were held together with copper rivets.

. . . that every year approximately twenty-seven thousand people are injured in fires in the United States and more than four thousand die in fires?

. . . that each year during the holiday season, some six hundred house fires are started by Christmas trees that catch fire because of faulty lights, candles, or sparks from fireplaces?

. . . that Boston had the first paid fire department in North America. In 1679, after a large fire, city leaders imported a fire engine from England and paid a fire chief and twelve firefighters to operate it.

. . . that a fire department responds to a fire somewhere in the United States every fifteen seconds?

. . . that the *fire triangle* denotes the three elements needed for fire? It consists of fuel (something to burn), heat (something to ignite the fuel), and air (oxygen). All three elements must be present to have a fire. A fire will burn until one or more of the elements is removed.

Related Professions

You don't actually have to enter burning buildings to be involved with fire fighting. The professionals on these pages have chosen to specialize in work that relates to fire fighting but takes place farther afield. Captain Sam Tsu (large photo, facing page) of the Montgomery County Fire Department in Maryland conducts an investigation in a charred living room. Was the fire caused by an electrical short or careless smoking? Or did someone set it on purpose?

Fire investigators look into the causes of fires that involve loss of life or significant property damage. They interview witnesses to the fire and prepare reports for police and for insurance companies. They are the front line of defense against arsonists, criminals who start fires to hurt people and/or ruin their property.

In the top photo at right, pilot Keith Laudert flies a tanker plane to practice a fire-retardant drop above the Montana wilderness. He works for Neptune, Inc., a private company that operates eight retardant planes. This plane can drop twenty-two thousand pounds of fire retardant. He can maneuver the plane to within about two hundred feet of the ground, so the retardant can be placed where it's most needed.

Doctors also specialize in helping people injured by fire. Dr. James Jeng (center right), a burn specialist, checks on a patient at the Washington Hospital Center in Washington, D.C.

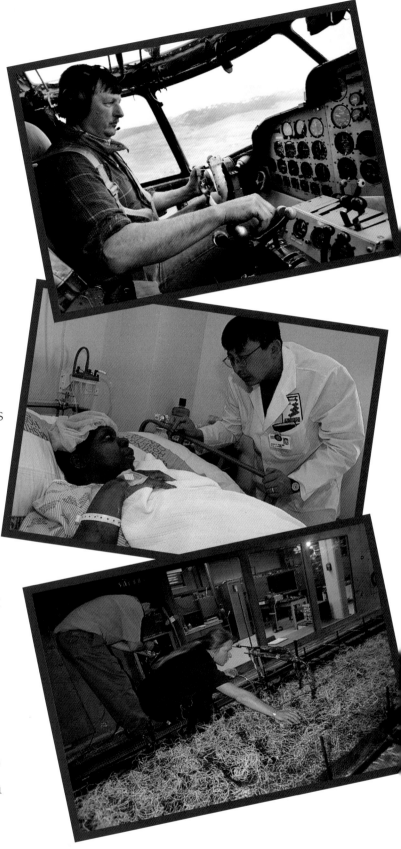

Fire science. *Scientists at the Missoula Fire Research Center (above) test the flammability of different wood chips. Their research will help foresters choose the most fire-resistant trees to plant when they reforest burned-out areas.*

Danger zone. *What's cooking? A toaster tart. The photo at right should remind you never to leave cooking food unattended. Not surprisingly, the majority of house fires begin in the kitchen. Here, researcher Larry Anderson, who works for Failure Analysis, Inc., a company in Menlo Park, California, conducts a flame test to see how long it takes for this seemingly harmless combination—a toaster and a pastry— to start a dangerous fire. A technician stands by with a fire extinguisher, in case the experiment burns out of control.*

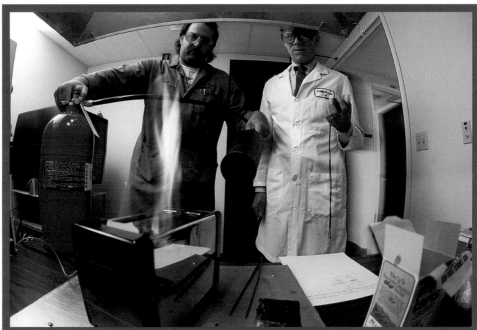

Twister! *The Laguna Canyon fire in Thousand Oaks, California, in October 1993, was already scary and dangerous. Then its swirling winds spawned a tornado (above). The fire destroyed 389 homes and burned 14,337 acres of land. California experiences cycles of fire and rain each year. Sometimes dry conditions and high winds cause natural brushfires to burn out of control and threaten homes. When large-scale disasters happen, many organizations rally together to help. During the fire shown in the large photo at right, firefighters from the U.S. Forest Service, and from the Los Angeles County and Los Angeles City Fire Departments, cooperated to cope with the dangerous situation.*

Famous Disasters

When disasters do occur, firefighters are ready to help control the devastation. On this page, emergency vehicles and personnel stand by as a helicopter makes a water drop near the mouth of Topanga Canyon in Malibu, California. Devastating fires and mud slides hit California in 1993. The state's annual cycle of fire and flood means that California firefighters must have emergency evacuation plans in place to rescue residents in dangerous situations.

In the inset photo at top left, rescue workers race against time to locate and dig out survivors of the Oklahoma City bombing in 1995. In 1997 terrible floods struck Grand Forks, North Dakota. As if that wasn't bad enough, broken gas lines fueled huge fires. Firefighters had to work in hip-deep water to save the city's historic downtown (inset photo, center). In the inset photo at bottom left, airport firefighters extinguish a blaze after a commercial airliner crash-landed just after takeoff at John F. Kennedy Airport in New York in 1992. All 293 passengers and crew members on board the TWA jet survived.

International Fire Fighting

Some disasters are so devastating they capture the attention of the whole world: earthquakes and mudslides; hurricanes and tornadoes; floods—and fires.

These pages reveal oil wells burning in the deserts of the Middle East, huge fires raging in the rainforests of Indonesia, and Britain's Windsor Castle engulfed in flames. When events like these happen, firefighters rush in to help.

In 1991 Iraqi soldiers retreating after the gulf war ignited some six hundred oil wells in retaliation for the bombing of Iraq. The fires created

black plumes of smoke that could be seen for miles, and caused an economic and environmental disaster. The burning wells were also a tough fire-fighting challenge. Experts from around the world arrived to help put out the fires and cap the wells. They sprayed foam on well fires and used huge tanks such as the one pictured above, capable of rolling over sand to blast retardant over the burning oil. In the small photo at left, you can see what a dirty job this can be! This firefighter is drenched in crude oil after trying to close a spewing well that had been damaged.

In 1997 fires in Indonesia's dense rainforest caused widespread environmental damage. The fires began when blazes set by farmers to clear fields veered out of control. Some five thousand people suffered smoke-related illness. The smoke blocked out the sun for weeks. More than three hundred thousand acres of forest in Indonesia were destroyed. At top right, a plantation worker tries to fight fire with fire by burning away the blaze's fuel—undergrowth.

The threat of fire exists even in one of the world's most protected landmarks. In November 1992 fire tore through Windsor Castle (right) which has been one of England's most important royal residences since the ninth century. The blaze destroyed large parts of the castle's interior, but its collection of priceless antique furniture and artwork—including drawings by Leonardo da Vinci—was carried to safety. Among the volunteers helping to save the treasures was a member of the Royal Family, Prince Andrew.

Climbing skills. *Firefighters in Japan, where earthquakes and fires are major threats, take their training seriously. In the photo at left they practice rope skills that may be required in rescues. The Japanese government takes fires seriously, too—a person can be sentenced to life in prison for carelessness that causes a severe fire.*

Famous Firefighters

Firefighters contribute to the quality of life for *all* residents in our communities—but too often they are recognized only by the people whose lives they save. On these pages meet some individuals whose special contributions to fire fighting have changed the ways that blazes are fought.

JOHN NELSON GAMEWELL
This manufacturer, who lived from 1822–1896, founded the company whose name was synonymous with the fire alarm (a device invented by Dr. William Channing in 1857). In the late 1800s, nearly every alarm box–telegraph system in use on city streets around the world bore the Gamewell name.

PATRICK H. RAYMOND
As the first African American fire chief, Raymond led firefighters who worked in Cambridge, Massachusetts, during the 1870s. He was also the first black member of the National Association of Fire Engineers, which was founded in 1873 and which later became the International Association of Fire Chiefs.

EDWARD C. PULASKI
This forest ranger saved the lives of thirty-four firefighters during a wildland fire in Idaho in 1910. Today, wildland firefighters rely on the Pulaski fire ax, a hand tool named in his honor. The ax has an edge for chopping at one end and an edge for digging at the other, a design that comes in handy in the woods.

DAVID GODWIN
In the 1930s Godwin, a pioneer smokejumper, was instrumental in encouraging the U.S. Forest Service to fly firefighters with parachutes into hard-to-reach wildfires. This approach was so effective in controlling wildland fires that specially trained firefighters have been leaping from planes ever since.

JAMES G. QUINTIERE
Dr. Quintiere heads the Fire Science and Engineering Division of the National Institute of Standards and Technology in Gaithersburg, Maryland. His recent study on the effect of gravity on fire behavior could help in developing fire-safe materials for use in the gravity-free environment of outer space.

TED PUTNAM
This wildland fire-fighting specialist developed the fire shelter, an aluminum-foil and fiberglass blanket that can be pulled over the body to protect a firefighter from wildfire flames. Putnam is a researcher and equipment specialist at the Missoula Technology and Development Center in Montana.

PAUL NEAL "RED" ADAIR
This legendary fighter of oil-well fires became a household name after the gulf war. Adair, of Houston, Texas, went to Kuwait to organize the battle to put out oil-well fires set by retreating Iraqi troops. In his 35-year career, Red extinguished 2,000 fires—an average of more than one a week. He retired in 1994.

RONALD HARUTO WAKIMOTO
Professor Wakimoto of the University of Montana School of Forestry in Missoula, Montana, specializes in wildland fire management. Dr. Wakimoto believes that controlled fires—or "prescribed burns"— are crucial to the health of our forests. He has testified before Congress about the best wildfire management techniques.

GENOIS WILSON
Wilson pioneered the first fire-safety program for deaf children and was among the first African American women who became professional firefighters. She is a district fire chief in Fort Wayne, Indiana.

ALFRED K. WHITEHEAD
After retiring as a captain of the Los Angeles fire department in 1988, Whitehead was elected general president of the International Association of Firefighters. He has worked to implement tough safety rules to protect firefighters.

JUDITH LIVERS BREWER
In 1973 Brewer, of Arlington, Virginia, became the first American woman—and one of the first women in the world—to become a professional firefighter. She has spoken in the United States and Europe about women's strengths as firefighters.

You Can Be a Firefighter!

The next time you hear the wail of a fire engine's siren, you may wonder whether the firefighters are heading to a blaze or a medical emergency—or if the alert is a false alarm. Will they encounter a hazardous-materials spill or a dangerous apartment-building fire? Will they have to put their lives on the line?

As you read this book, you may have discovered that working as a firefighter is a lot more complicated than just spraying water on flames. Fire fighting is a career that takes courage and strength, daring and decision-making skills.

At right, twin brothers Kyle and Jason Neumann, age twelve, of Herndon, Virginia, hope to become firefighters one day. Jason (left) and Kyle wear fire-fighting gear that's still a bit too big for them, but they're already familiar with the demands of the job because their dad, Ken Neumann, is a firefighter at Fire Station No. 36 in Fairfax County, Virginia. The twins have spent time at the station with their dad, and have even ridden on the fire truck. Kyle and Jason know about the long hours and the danger of the job. They also know that firefighters take tremendous pride in their work and forge deep friendships with their colleagues.

If you can imagine fighting flames, rescuing accident victims, helping sick people—even parachuting into trees to douse a wilderness fire—then you may have what it takes to be a firefighter. You would be joining a proud tradition of men and women who are willing to put their own lives at risk to protect others. It's not too soon to get started. To find out how to get more information about this exciting and essential job, turn the page.

Other Sources of Information

PROFESSIONAL FIRE-FIGHTING ORGANIZATIONS

International Association of Fire Chiefs (IAFC)
4025 Fair Ridge Drive
Fairfax, VA 22033

This group provides information and education services to career and volunteer chiefs and to managers of emergency services organizations throughout the world.

International Association of Fire Fighters (IAFF)
1750 New York Avenue, NW,
Third Floor
Washington, DC 20006

Founded in 1918, this organization is dedicated to the welfare of its 225,000 member firefighters. The IAFF also produces educational materials for young people interested in careers in fire fighting.

National Fire Protection Association (NFPA)
1 Batterymarch Park
Quincy, MA 02269

The NFPA, which was organized in 1896, works to reduce the burden of fire by advocating scientifically based codes and standards, research, and education for fire and related safety issues. The association publishes the National Fire Codes and the Learn Not to Burn curriculum.

National Smokejumper Association (NSA)
P.O. BOX 4081
Missoula, MT 59806

This association's purpose is to establish, develop, sustain, and maintain the traditions and esprit de corps of all smokejumpers and associate members in the national organization. It publishes four newsletters a year.

The National Volunteer Fire Council
1050 17th Street, NW, Suite 1212
Washington, DC 20036

This association represents volunteer fire services, emergency medical services, and rescue services throughout the United States.

GOVERNMENT AGENCIES

Federal Emergency Management Agency (FEMA)
Federal Center Plaza
500 C Street, SW
Washington, DC 20472

This national agency coordinates responses to emergencies such as earthquakes, hurricanes, floods, and other natural disasters.

U.S. Consumer Product Safety Commission (CPSC)
330 East West Highway
Bethesda, Maryland 20814

This organization reports on the safety of products available to the public, including fire equipment such as smoke detectors and extinguishers.

U.S. Fire Administration (USFA)
16825 South Seton Avenue
Emmitsburg, MD 21727

The USFA provides national leadership in fire training, data collection, technology and public education, and awareness, supporting the efforts of local communities to save lives and reduce injuries and property that result from fires.

National Interagency Fire Center (NIFC)
3833 South Development Avenue
Boise, ID 83705

The NIFC is the nation's primary support center for wildland fire suppression. It works with state and local agencies to provide national response to wildfires and other emergencies and serves as a center for wildland fire information and technology.

SAFETY ORGANIZATIONS

Burn Prevention Foundation
5000 Tilghman Street
Allentown, PA 18104

National Fire Safety Council
4065 Page Avenue
Michigan Center, MI 49254

National SAFE KIDS Campaign
1301 Pennsylvania Avenue, NW,
Suite 1000
Washington, DC 20004

National Safety Council
1121 Spring Lake Drive
Itasca, IL 60143

A SAMPLING OF FIRE MUSEUMS

Fire Museum of Maryland
1301 York Road
Lutherville, MD 21093

This museum houses sixty pieces of fire equipment dating from 1822 to 1957 as well as a working fire alarm–telegraph display.

Fire Museum of Texas
400 Walnut Street
Beaumont, TX 77701

This museum offers a learn-by-doing center on fire prevention as well as exhibits of historic equipment.

The Firehouse Museum
1572 Columbia Street
San Diego, CA 92101

This museum displays a large collection of fire-fighting equipment from throughout the United States and the world.

Fireman's Hall
147 N. 2d Street
Philadelphia, PA 19106

Housed in an 1876 firehouse, this museum details the history of fire fighting in America—starting with Philadelphia's own Ben Franklin.

Hall of Flame
6101 East Van Buren Street
Phoenix, AZ 85008

One of the largest of the approximately 150 fire museums in the United States, this museum has many pieces of historic fire equipment and a large firefighting library.

New York City Fire Museum
278 Spring Street
New York, New York 10013

The museum houses memorabilia, including fire engines from Colonial times to the present, in a firehouse built in 1904.

Smithsonian Institution
1000 Jefferson Drive, SW
Washington, DC 20560

The collections of America's national museum include a significant array of antique fire apparatus.

PHOTO CREDITS